Aural Time!

Practice Tests for ABRSM and other Exams

Grade 8

DAVID TURNBULL

CONTENTS

Introduction	ii
Test A: Singing or Playing from Memory, Cadences and Chords	1
Test B: Sight Singing	7
Test C: Modulations	12
Test D: Discussing musical features	18

Bosworth

14/15 Berners Street, London W1T 3LJ

INTRODUCTION

Aural training has always been of the greatest importance to teachers and their pupils. In recent years the emphasis has changed from dependence on memory to the development of a wider sense of musical awareness.

The Associated Board of the Royal Schools of Music revised its aural tests for Grades 1–5 in 1993 (with some further changes in Grades 4 and 5 in 1995). New tests were introduced for Grades 6 to 8 in January, 1996.

Like most musical skills, aural awareness needs regular training and practice. Aural work should be part of every lesson. Teachers may like to use this book to supplement the aural training material they devise for themselves.

The 1996 tests for Grade 8 include tests in sight singing a melody below a played upper part. Sight singing of any sort — the basis of so much musical training and enjoyment — has been neglected in musical education in the last few decades. Pupils will therefore need considerable practice to achieve the necessary standard. Pupils may be also find another book in the *Aural Time!* series useful. *Easy Sight Singing & Voice Pitching Practice*, (Bosworth Edition 4801), contains 70 short examples of accompanied sight-singing suitable for a beginner, in a variety of major and minor keys.

The material in these books is not intended only for ABRSM examinations. The skills developed by their use will be of considerable help to candidates for GCSE and A level, and for all musicians who wish to improve their general musical awareness.

Most of the examples have been taken from the works of established composers. However, in many cases examples have been adapted or transposed to make them more useful for their present purpose. This is particularly true of examples which have to be sung.

As the *Aural Time!* series reaches its end, I must record my thanks to some of those who have helped me. My wife, in particular, has spent much time proof-reading and playing over examples, and has been a constant source of encouragement. Howard Friend, Editor and a director of Bosworth & Co., has been patient and ever-helpful. Paul Terry, of Musonix, has not only done the typesetting of the later books most beautifully, but has always been ready to put his musicological skill at my disposal. John Leach has also given me valuable help. I am grateful to all these musicians: the imperfections which remain in the books are mine and not theirs.

David Turnbull
Solihull, January 1996

Uniform with this volume: *Aural Time!* Grades 1–7. Pupil's book for Grades 4 & 5, and Grades 6, 7 and 8 (in preparation).

Compact Discs with recordings of tests from *Aural Time!* Grades 6, 7 and 8 are also in preparation.

Also by David Turnbull: *Theory Time!* Step-by-step instruction in musical theory and rudiments. Grades 1–5.

All published by Bosworth & Co.

Test 8A

There are **three sections** to this test.

i. The pupil must *sing or play from memory* the *lowest* part of a three-part phrase (marked ⌐⎯⎯⌐) played twice. Before each playing the key-chord and starting note must be played and named, and the pulse indicated.

ii. The pupil must *name* the cadence at the end of a second (following) phrase as perfect, plagal, imperfect or interrupted. This second phrase must be played *twice*, preceded each time by its key-chord.

iii. The key-chord must be sounded once more, and the cadence chords (marked *) played. These must then be played a second time, **with a pause on each**, so that the pupil can name the chords. The chords which may be used are:

> the tonic (root position, first inversion or second inversion);
> the supertonic (root position or first inversion);
> the subdominant (root position);
> the dominant (root position, first inversion or second inversion);
> the dominant seventh (root position);
> the submediant (root position).

Chords may be described either as above, or by using Roman notation.

© 1996 by Bosworth & Co. Ltd., London

International Copyright Secured

Test B. Sight-Singing

Pupils must sing at sight the lower part of a two-part passage, the upper part being played for them by the teacher or examiner. The passage can be in any major or minor key up to and including those with four sharps or four flats. The key-chord and the starting note will be played, and the pulse indicated.

In examinations, candidates may choose to sing a passage in *either* the treble *or* the bass clef. **In practice sessions pupils are strongly advised to use both clefs, to increase their familiarity with them.**

In examinations, a second attempt may be allowed. When practising, pupils should repeat the test as often as necessary to get a correct performance.

Test C. Modulations.

In Grade 7, pupils learned to recognise modulations from a major key to the keys of its dominant, subdominant and relative minor. In addition to these, in Grade 8 pupils must be able to recognise modulation from a major key to its supertonic key.

Pupils must also be able to recognise a modulation from a minor key to its dominant minor, dominant major, subdominant minor and relative major.

It may be helpful for pupils to practise these preliminary exercises, by C. H. Kitson. Pupils should listen to them, and if possible play them over – if pupils are not keyboard players, recommend them to sing or play each part over separately.

Test D. Discussing musical features

The approach to Test D in Grade 8 is somewhat different from that adopted in the earlier grades, in which questions were asked about musical features *specified by the examiner*.

In Grade 8, comments will be invited about particular features of the music *which the candidate finds interesting*.

The comments of the candidate may lead to a discussion of other features, leading to a decision about the style and period of the music and a possible composer (see the *Notes on historical periods* in the Pupils' Books for *Aural Time!* Grades 6–8. Teachers may also like to draw the attention of pupils to the notes *Listening to musical features* in the same books. These should provide starting points for comments.)

In the event of difficulty, examiners may prompt candidates about certain areas of interest.

It will be seen from *Listening to musical features* that there are eight main areas:

Rhythm (including Tempo);
Melody;
Tonality;
Dynamics;
Articulation;
Harmony;
Texture;
Form.

It will help pupils if they memorise these.

The approach to music needed for Test D in Grade 8 will be found of great use to pupils, not only for practical examinations but for many others, including GCSE, A level Music and the A level General Paper and similar examinations. It is also a vital part of general education, and the general approach can be transferred to other fields.

Examples from Test D sections, with their notes, in *Aural Time!* Grades 6 and 7 can be used for further practice.

Brief comments about the music in this section will be found below each example. *Pupils should be reminded that these comments and opinions are not the only possible ones. They may wish to add others of their own, but must always be prepared to justify their comments with evidence from the music.*

D1 (Chopin: *Cantabile in B♭ major*). Possible subjects for discussion include:

Tempo	A gentle andante, with some rubato. In last line, a *rallentando* and a dying away.
Melodic phrases	First phrase concludes with an imperfect cadence; a modified repeat of this ends with a perfect cadence. The rest of the piece is a coda over a tonic pedal, consisting of a shorter phrase, repeated, rounded off by tonic chords decorated with appoggiaturas.
Articulation	Legato and *cantabile* melodic line until the final chords.
Dynamics	Use of *cresc.* and *dim.* throughout. Coda very soft and dies away at the end.
Tonality and Harmony	Major key and essentially without modulation – but there are many secondary 7ths and other **chromatic** chords. Final section (last 6 bars) has a **tonic pedal**.
Texture	Homophonic: the free and expressive melodic line supported by steady left-hand broken chords spanning a wide range is characteristic of a **Nocturne**.

All these features suggest piano music of the Romantic period, particularly Chopin.

D2 (Byrd: *Victoria*). Possible subjects for discussion include:

Form	Two sections of equal length. The second is a **variation** of the first.
Metre	Simple triple, with **hemiola** (e.g. bars 6–7) and **syncopation** (bars 5 and 8).
Tempo	Consistent steady pulse. The second section seems faster than the first because of the **divisions** of the beats.
Melodic phrases	Mainly conjunct. Long notes in the first section. The second half is a variation of the first, using much shorter note lengths.
Dynamics	All at the same level.
Tonality, etc.	Major key: both sections modulate to the subdominant, and from there straight to the dominant.
Harmony	Mostly triads in root-position and first position. Suspensions at the cadences in the first section and many inessential notes in the second section.
Texture	Mainly homophonic, but some contrapuntal movement in the tenor part of the second section.

The lack of contrast in the dynamics, the triadic harmony and the way in which chords of long duration are decorated suggest keyboard music (for Virginals or Harpsichord) of the late Renaissance or early Baroque period.

D3 (Liszt: No. 3 of *Four Little Piano Pieces*). Possible subjects for discussion include:

Tempo	A slow tempo, with *ritardandi* and pauses at the end of the second and final sections.
Form	Ternary. An opening phrase, repeated with modification to cadence in the dominant. Middle section based on the falling figure from this cadence. Final section similar to first, but with thicker texture and change of key.
Articulation	Legato throughout.
Dynamics	Quiet, but with some modification at the end of the central section.
Tonality, etc.	Major, with modulations to related keys. There is an unexpected modulation (a **tertiary** modulation – here, up a major 3rd from F♯ to A major) at the start of the final section but this ends back in the tonic key.
Harmony	Mostly diatonic harmony but notice the diminished 7th that ends the central section.
Texture	It starts with a homophonic two-part texture, in thirds and sixths, then progressively thickens. The middle section is imitative.
Character	Contemplative, almost like church music.
	The changes in tempo, use of sustaining pedal, pause on a diminished 7th and tertiary modulation suggest piano music of the Romantic period.

Reproduced by kind permission of the publisher
J. W. Chester / Edition Wilhelm Hansen, London

D4 (Stravinsky: No. 1 from *Les Cinq Doigts*). Possible subjects for discussion include:

Melody	Narrow range, with some feeling of folksong. Mostly **conjunct**, but a rising 4th is a feature of the middle section.
Rhythm	Simple: no dotted notes, syncopation or irregular patterns.
Metre	Simple duple, but with a single bar of triple metre in the first (and last) section.
Form	Ternary, with exact repeat of A section.
Dynamics	No variety.
Tonality, etc.	Major; entirely diatonic.
Harmony	Non-functional **diatonic harmony** with frequent dissonance. Middle section is based on a dominant pedal.
Texture	Mostly two- and three-part homophonic, but with a little independence of parts later. The entire piece uses a relatively high texture.

The constant use of unprepared dissonance suggests early twentieth century piano music.

D5 (Grieg: *Poetic Tone Picture* Op.3 No. 5, first section). Possible subjects for discussion include:

Phrase structure	The extract consists of two musical sentences. The first consists of a phrase (bars 1-4) that is repeated in **sequence** (bars 5-8) a third lower. The second is a varied restatement of the first, starting louder and with a short extension to end in the tonic.
Tempo and rhythm	A fast speed, with a *rit.* at the end of the extract. The accompaniment, in particular, features **syncopation**.
Dynamics	Contrasted: a quiet start and end, but a loud restatement of the main theme in the middle.
Articulation	Particularly strong accents on the first beats of some of the bars.
Tonality	Major key, with some **chromaticism** (particularly at phrase endings).
Harmony	7ths, 9ths, chromatic chords and short pedal points help make the harmony quite complex.
Texture	Predominantly chordal and quite thick: in the second half the bass is mainly an octave lower and the open fifths (now with crushed notes) are more prominent.

The rich harmony, chromaticism, syncopation and frequent use of the sustaining pedal all suggest piano music of the Romantic period.

D6 (Beethoven: Bagatelle, Op. 119 No, 11). Possible subjects for discussion include:

Form and Texture	Two *cantabile* sections, separated by a two-bar link, and concluded with a short coda. The first section has a repeated four-bar melody, supported by simple chords, followed by a two-bar phrase in similar style and texture which is then repeated up a tone in free **sequence**. The second section has a new four-bar melody, sounded high on the piano with a chordal accompaniment. This is repeated an octave lower with much greater independence of parts. The four-bar coda is strictly **homophonic**.

Dynamics	Predominantly *p* but with some variation.
Tonality	Major, with brief modulations to related keys in the second half of the first section only.
Harmony	Straightforward, **functional** harmony. The diatonic opening is built around an inner **pedal** on the dominant. A diminished 7th introduces the chromatic link.
Character	Restrained and contemplative. The outer sections are almost hymn-like, but the diminished 7th heralds a change of mood to legato melody contrasting with detached accompaniment.

The functional harmony and periodic phrasing point to the Classical style, with some romantic elements. Early 19th Century in period.

Reproduced by permission of Editions Alphonse Leduc, Paris / United Music Publishers Ltd.

D7 (Jehan Alain: *En dévissant mes chaussettes*, No. 9 of *Dix Pièces pour Piano*, 1931). Possible subjects for discussion include:

Metre	No fixed metre to this piece (it is **ametric**, or 'in free time'), but it flows continuously.
Melody	Mainly descending scales with an even crotchet (quarter note) rhythm that permeates almost the entire piece. (The bass has a long descending scale in minims).
Texture	Basically four-part counterpoint, with **canonic imitation** between treble and tenor voices.
Dynamics	Piano at the start, a small climax at the forte in the middle, and dying away to a piano end.
Tempo	No change other than (possibly) a slight *rit.* at the end.
Tonality, etc.	The lack of conventional cadences gives the music a modal quality, although there is a feeling of tonal centres that progress from major to relative minor through the course of the piece. The ending is tonally ambiguous, with a chromatic chord and major-minor conflict over a tonic pedal.

The metrical freedom, modality and diatonic dissonance (together with tonally ambiguous ending), suggest an early Twentieth Century date.

D8 (Pachelbel: Fugue). Possible subjects for discussion include:

Texture & form	A four-voice **fugue**, although the contrapuntal texture is often in just two or three parts.
Dynamics	No change in the level of dynamic (other than that caused by differences in texture).
Tempo	No change other than (possibly) a slight *rit.* at the end.
Tonality, etc.	Major key, with brief modulations to nearly-related keys only. There is a very short chromatic passage in the middle.
Rhythm	Constant driving pulse of short note-lengths, with much repetition of rhythmic patterns.
	The fugal texture, **monothematicism** (use of a single theme) and driving rhythm all suggest Baroque keyboard music.

D9 (Hanns Jelinek: *Charakterstück* from *Zwölftonwerk*, Op. 15/2). Possible subjects for discussion include:

Melodic shape	Angular (**disjunct** motion), with wide leaps in many places.
Form	An arch form, in which a central climax is differentiated by dynamic, texture, pitch range and articulation. The opening material re-appears in free inversion in the last three bars.
Texture	Two-part texture throughout. The treble and bass are in **dialogue** for most of the piece, coming together briefly at the central climax.

(continued on page 28)

Dynamics	A long crescendo from the start to the central climax, and then a quiet ending. There is wide variation in the dynamic level.
Articulation	Legato (distubed by off-beat accents) in the outer sections; heavily accented at the climax.
Tempo	Quite fast, but with frequent changes (fastest at the central climax).
Tonality, etc.	**Atonal** (no fixed key centre) and therefore not in any major or minor scale. (Actually dodecaphonic though a pupil would be unlikely to gasp this on one hearing.)
Harmony	Dissonant in many places.
	The dissonance and extremes of expression suggest a mid-Twentieth Century date.

D10 (Bach: Prelude, BWV 931). Possible subjects for discussion include:

Texture	Mainly three-part writing: the bass has considerable contrapuntal independence but the two top parts are often in parallel thirds. There is significant ornamentation in all parts.
Dynamics	No change in the level of dynamics.
Tempo	A steady pulse, which doesn't change other than (possibly) a slight *rit*. at the end.
Tonality, etc.	Minor key, but with a **tierce de picardie** at the end, so it finishes on a major *chord*. There are brief modulations in the central part of the piece.
Harmony	Basically simple chords are highly decorated with suspensions and appoggiaturas.
	The contrapuntal texture, along with the melodic and harmonic decoration, suggest keyboard music of the late Baroque, and particularly Bach.

D11 (Haydn: Minuet from Sonata in F.) Possible subjects for discussion include:

Form	**Binary** form minuet. The B section is longer than the A section and begins with a variant of the opening melody, transferred to the bass.
Melody	The main theme is characterised by an upward leap followed by a descending scale. This two-bar phrase is repeated in **sequence** and then answered by a four-bar phrase modulating to the dominant. The entire piece is constructed from similarly regular (**periodic**) phrases. Generally, the melody has a wide range and is frequently decorated.
Texture	Thin, melody-dominated texture, often in just two parts.
Dynamics	No changes in the level of dynamics.
Tempo and Rhythm	A steady pulse. All phrases are characterised by an up-beat (**anacrusic**) start.
Tonality, etc.	Major key, modulating to the dominant in the middle.
Harmony	**Functional** harmony, with a little chromatic decoration and a number of suspensions and appoggiaturas.

The melody-dominated texture, functional harmony, periodic phrasing and melodic decoration all suggest a minuet in the Classical style.

D12 (Rameau: first part of *Tambourin* from *Pièces de Clavecin*, 1724) Possible subjects for discussion include:

Form	**Rondo**: three refrains separated by two quieter episodes (ABACA).
Melody	The refrain consists of two nearly identical phrases, differing only in that the first ends with an imperfect cadence while the second ends with a perfect cadence. The melody of the first episode is similar to the refrain, but it begins an octave higher. The melody of the second episode is **chromatic**. Ornamentation with **mordents** occurs throughout.
Texture	Melody with chordal accompaniment.
Dynamics	Sharply contrasted by section (**terraced** dynamics).
Tempo and Rhythm	Fast, duple time and regular phrase lengths suggesting a dance movement: the rhythmic structure is that of a **gavotte**.
Tonality, etc.	Minor key, without modulation, but with a chromatic passage in the second episode.
Harmony	Almost entirely tonic and dominant chords, apart from the chromatic section. There is a tonic **pedal** throughout (a double pedal, or drone bass, in the A and B sections).
	The driving rhythm, simple harmony, terraced dynamics, monothematicism and constant ornamentation all suggest a *gavotte en rondeau* in the French Baroque style.